THE CLASSIC DESSERT RECIPES COOKBOOK

50 HEALTHY DESSERT RECIPES

FRANKLIN GOODWIN

Table of Contents

INTRODUCTION

A "dessert" is a course of food served after dinner. Dessert foods are typically sweet, but they can also be powerfully flavored dishes, such as cheese, as in cheese cake. Dessert is derived from the Old French term "desservir," which means "to clean the table." Dessert is frequently confused with the word desert (notice the single "s"), which refers to a bare piece of land with sand as the soil.

The emergence of the middle class and the industrialization of the sugar business did not bring the privilege of sweets to the general people until the 19th century, when it was no longer reserved for the nobility or as a rare holiday treat. This was because sugar became more affordable and accessible to the general populace. Desserts developed and became popular as sugar became more commonly available.

Dessert dishes have been a common topic of conversation in today's culture, as they are a great way to win people over at the end of any dinner. This is largely because if you serve a mediocre lunch but a great dessert, people would remember you for the dessert rather than the meal.

Some of the most common desserts are:

- biscuits or biscuits
- Ice
- meringue
- fruit
- Cake
- Crumbles
- Vanilla pudding
- Gelatin desserts
- pudding
- pastries
- cakes or pies

DESSERT RECIPES

1. Strawberry and mint sorbet

ingredients

- 250 g strawberries (fresh)
- 120 ml sugar syrup (1 part water boiled down with 1 part sugar)
- 1/2 orange (juice and zest)
- 1/2 lemon (juice)
- 15 mint leaves
- Melissa leaves (for garnish)
- Mint leaves (for garnish)

preparation

1. For the strawberry and mint sorbet, wash and clean the strawberries and remove the stems. Chop the mint leaves and mix finely with all the other ingredients. Freeze the mixture in the ice cream maker or pour it into a shallow tub and freeze while stirring repeatedly.

2. Use a spoon dipped in hot water to prick the dumplings and serve in small glass bowls or suitable glasses. Garnish the strawberry and mint sorbet with mint or lemon balm leaves.

2. Quick chestnut dessert

ingredients

- 1 orange
- 1 teaspoon granulated sugar
- 1 teaspoon cinnamon

For the chestnut cream:

- 250 g chestnut rice
- 2 tbsp milk
- 150 g mascarpone
- 60 g icing sugar
- 1 tbsp rum
- 200 g whipped cream

For the garnish:

- 100 g cocoa powder (unsweetened)

- 4 teaspoons brittle
- 1 orange (in columns)
- 4 chestnuts (peeled, cooked)

preparation

1. Wash the orange thoroughly. Rub the skin, then fillet the pulp. Sprinkle the orange fillets with granulated sugar and cinnamon.
2. Remove 4 tbsp chestnut rice. Puree the remaining amount with milk until smooth. Whip the whipped cream until stiff.
3. Mix the mascarpone with the chestnut puree, sugar, rum and 1 teaspoon orange peel until fluffy. Add whipped cream.
4. Pour 1 tablespoon of the removed chestnut rice into dessert glasses, spread some orange fillets on top and fill the glasses with chestnut cream. Dust the surface thickly with cocoa powder, sprinkle with brittle and garnish with orange wedges and whole chestnuts to taste.
5. Chill until ready to serve.

3. Crispy dessert with banana and Brazil nuts

ingredients

- 400 g banana yogurt
- 200 g crunchy muesli
- 150 ml milk
- 3 bananas (small)
- 100 g Brazil nuts
- 50 ml maple syrup

preparation

1. Soak the muesli in the milk for about 15 minutes.
2. Chop the Brazil nuts and toast them in a heated pan without fat. Add maple syrup, stir briefly and remove from heat.

3. Peel the bananas and cut into small pieces. Save some slices for decoration. Mix the banana slices with the nut and maple mixture.
4. Strain the muesli, pour into bowls, spread the nut-banana mixture on top, garnish with banana yoghurt and a few pieces of banana.

4. Grill pineapple

ingredients

- 5 allspice grains
- 15 g whole cane sugar (1 tbsp)
- 4 tbsp desiccated coconut
- 1 pineapple
- 2 tbsp oil
- 1 tbsp maple syrup

Preparation steps

1. Crush the allspice in a mortar and mix with the sugar.
2. Toast the coconut flakes in a pan without fat. Let cool on a plate.

3. Peel the pineapple, cut into 2 cm thick slices and brush with a little oil.
4. Grill the pineapple slices on the very hot grill briefly on each side and sprinkle with the allspice sugar after turning. Place the pineapple slices on a plate. Drizzle the fruit slices with the syrup and sprinkle with the coconut flakes.

5. Tofu chocolate mousse

ingredients

- 100 g dark chocolate (at least 70% cocoa)
- 1 small organic orange
- 1 vanilla pod
- 80 g coconut blossom sugar
- 700 g silken tofu
- 40 g cocoa powder
- 3 tbsp cooled espresso
- 2 proteins
- salt

Preparation steps

1. Roughly chop the chocolate.

2. Melt the chocolate in a bowl over a hot, but not boiling, water bath.
3. Rinse orange with hot water, rub dry and finely rub the peel. (Use the fruit elsewhere.)
4. Halve the vanilla pod lengthways, scrape out the pulp and mix with the coconut blossom sugar.
5. Beat the tofu, cocoa powder, orange peel, vanilla sugar and espresso with the whisk of the hand mixer or in the food processor until creamy.
6. Pour the chocolate into the tofu mixture and stir until smooth.
7. Separate the eggs (use the yolks otherwise). Beat the egg whites with a pinch of salt using the hand mixer whisk.
8. Fold the egg whites under the tofu mixture. Pour the mousse into glasses and chill for 2 hours.

6. Quick berry ice cream

ingredients

- 350 g mixed berries (frozen)
- ½ lemon
- 125 ml buttermilk
- 1 tsp cinnamon
- 4 tbsp liquid honey
- 2 stems lemon balm

Preparation steps

1. Put the berries in a tall container and let thaw for about 5 minutes. In the meantime, squeeze 1-2 tablespoons of juice from the lemon.
2. Mix the buttermilk, cinnamon, honey and lemon juice.

3. Pour seasoned buttermilk over the berries and puree everything finely with a hand blender. Place ice in the freezer for 10 minutes. Cut balls with the ice cream scoop. Wash lemon balm, shake dry, pluck the leaves off and garnish the ice cream with them.

7. Yogurt cream with fruits

ingredients

- 250 g yogurt
- 2 tbsp icing sugar
- 1 lemon (juice)
- 2 sheets of gelatin
- 120 g cream (whipped (easiest in the office from a can))
- 100 g berries
- 1 pc kiwi
- 1 apple

preparation

1. For the yoghurt cream with fruits, soak gelatine sheets in cold water. Mix the yogurt

with lemon juice and sugar until smooth. Gently heat about 2 tablespoons of the yoghurt mixture in a small saucepan, dissolve the squeezed gelatine in it and stir into the yoghurt mixture. Fold in the whipped cream. Fill into deep plates or glasses and let cool briefly in the freezer. Peel the kiwi and cut into slices. Peel the apple as desired and cut into wedges. Distribute the berries and fruits decoratively on the cream.

8. Strawberry cold bowl

ingredients

- 250 g buttermilk
- 125 g whipped cream
- 125 g yogurt
- 250 g strawberries
- 3 tbsp sugar
- 1 squirt of lemon juice
- 1 teaspoon vanilla sugar

preparation

1. For the strawberry cold bowl, puree all the ingredients and half of the strawberries in a blender.

2. Halve the second half of the strawberries and mix with the pureed mass before serving. Carefully fold in the whipped cream.
3. Serve the strawberry cold bowl in bowls. Decorate with mint, chocolate flakes, pistachios or the like as you wish.

9. Strawberry Lasagna

ingredients

- 250 g mascarpone
- 1 pod of vanilla
- 150 g natural yogurt
- 250 ml whipped cream
- 1 kg of strawberries
- 1 Pkg. Ladyfingers
- 3 tbsp icing sugar

preparation

1. For the strawberry lasagna, cut open the vanilla pod and scrape it out. Mix the vanilla pulp well with the mascarpone and natural yoghurt. Whip the whipped cream until stiff and fold into the mixture.

2. Rinse and drain the strawberries. Cut 250 g of it into small pieces. Put one part in a baking dish as a base layer. Line the second layer with ladyfingers. Puree the rest of the strawberries with icing sugar and pour over the ladyfingers as a third layer. Layer the individual ingredients alternately as usual.
3. Then put the mold in the refrigerator for a few minutes. For the strawberry lasagna, grate the chocolate and sprinkle over it just before serving.

10. Chia pudding dessert

ingredients

- 3 tbsp chia seeds
- 100 ml almond milk (or rice milk, etc.)
- 100 g berries (mixed, possibly thawed frozen)
- 3 tbsp yogurt (10% fat)
- 4 tbsp oatmeal
- Berries (mixed, fresh)

preparation

1. For the chia pudding dessert, divide the chia seeds between 2 glasses or bowls and pour almond milk over them. Mix the milk and seeds well and let them soak in the

refrigerator for at least 30 minutes. In the meantime, puree the berries.

2. When the seeds are firm, spread a thin layer of oatmeal over them. Then carefully layer the puree and yogurt on top.

3. Garnish with fresh berries and serve.

11. Curd milk cold bowl

ingredients

- 600 g blueberries (fresh or frozen)
- 1 organic lemon
- 3 tbsp cane sugar
- 2 tbsp cassis or currant syrup
- 800 ml curdled milk
- 2 tbsp liquid honey
- 150 ml soy cream
- 30 g amaretti

Preparation steps

1. Wash blueberries, drain well; Thaw frozen foods. Rinse the lemon with hot water, rub

dry, finely grate the peel. Halve the lemon, squeeze out and measure 2 tablespoons of juice. Bring 2/3 of the blueberries, sugar and cassis or syrup to the boil in a saucepan. Cook on medium heat for 5 minutes.

2. Use a spoon to force the blueberries through a fine sieve into a bowl, squeezing out as much juice as possible.

3. Add the rest of the blueberries to the juice, set aside and allow to cool completely.

4. Beat the curd, honey, soy cream and lemon zest until smooth. Chill for 1 hour (or more). To serve, place the cold bowl in deep plates, place 1 serving of compote in the middle. Crumble the amaretti with your hands and sprinkle on top.

12. Blueberry and peach compote

ingredients

- 200 g blueberries
- 500 g ripe peaches (4 ripe peaches)
- 1 branch rosemary
- 4 tbsp maple syrup
- 1 protein
- 1 pinch
- salt
- 30 g sugar (1.5 tbsp)

Preparation steps

1. Sort the blueberries, wash, halve and stone the peaches. Put all the fruits in a baking dish.
2. Wash rosemary, shake dry and add.

3. Drizzle the maple syrup over it, seal the tin with aluminum foil and bake in a preheated oven at 180 ° C (convection: 160 ° C, gas: level 2-3) for 20 minutes.
4. Separate the egg (use the egg yolk otherwise), beat the egg white and salt in a tall vessel with the whisk of a hand mixer until the sugar drizzles in.
5. Remove the aluminum foil and spread the egg whites onto the fruit with a rubber spatula. Bake for another 8-10 minutes and serve immediately.

13. Lemon balm sorbet

ingredients

- ½ vanilla pod
- 1 organic lime
- 1 bunch lemon balm
- 50 g coconut blossom sugar (2.5 tbsp)
- 150 ml light grape juice vegan
- 400 g strawberries

Preparation steps

1. Cut half the vanilla pod lengthways and scrape out the pulp. Rinse the lime with hot, rub dry, halve and cut 1 half into slices.
2. Wash lemon balm and shake dry. Put 1-2 stems aside for the garnish, put the rest in a bowl.

3. Bring the vanilla pod and pulp, lime slices, coconut blossom sugar, grape juice and 450 ml water to the boil in a saucepan and dissolve the coconut blossom sugar completely while stirring.
4. Pour the sugar solution over the lemon balm and let it steep for 10–15 minutes. Then pour the liquid through a fine sieve into a flat baking dish and place in the freezer.
5. As soon as the liquid starts to freeze at the edge, stir everything well with a hand blender. Repeat the process frequently during the freezing time of 6 hours: the more often you stir, the finer the consistency.
6. Finely grate the peel of the remaining lime, squeeze out the juice and put both in a bowl.
7. Wash the strawberries carefully, pat dry, clean and cut into slices.
8. Mix with the lime zest and juice and let it steep in the refrigerator.
9. Shape the finished sorbet with a tablespoon and serve with the marinated strawberries. Garnish with the lemon balm set aside and serve.

14. Curd cheese cream with blueberries

ingredients

- 125 g curd cheese
- 1/3 cup sour cream (approx. 80g)
- 1 orange (juice)
- 1-2 tbsp icing sugar
- 1 pinch of vanilla sugar
- 200 g blueberries
- 2 tbsp rum
- 4 tbsp granulated sugar
- Hip (for garnish)

preparation

1. For the curd cheese cream, stir the curd cheese with the sour cream, orange juice, icing sugar and vanilla sugar until smooth.

Mash or mix about a third of the blueberries with the back of a spoon. Fold under the curd mixture.

2. Mix the remaining berries with rum and granulated sugar and heat lukewarm in a small saucepan. Pour berries into glasses. Spread the curd mixture over the top and garnish with ribs.

15. Chocolate mousse

ingredients

- 80 g dark chocolate couverture
- 1 egg white
- 1 teaspoon granulated sugar
- 125 ml whipped cream
- Cocoa powder (for sprinkling)

preparation

1. For the chocolate mousse, melt the chocolate in a snow kettle over steam. Take off the stove.
2. Beat the egg whites with sugar and fold into the chocolate. Beat the cream until half-firm, set aside 3 tablespoons for the garnish and fold the rest into the chocolate mixture.

3. Pour the chocolate mousse into decorative glasses. Garnish with the rest of the cream and chill briefly or serve immediately. Sprinkle with cocoa powder beforehand.

16. Plum roaster

ingredients

- 600 g plums (pitted)
- 300 g of sugar
- 2 cloves
- Cinnamon bark
- Lemon juice

preparation

1. First wash and stone the plums.
2. Then slowly simmer the plums with sugar, cloves, cinnamon bark, lemon juice and a little water until the plum skin curls slightly outwards.

3. Now remove from the heat and pour the plum roaster into glasses that have been rinsed with hot water.

17. Apple cider compote

ingredients

- 1.5kg of apples
- 1 l apple cider
- 250 grams of sugar
- Cloves
- 1 cinnamon bark
- Ziron juice (juice of 1 lemon)

preparation

1. For the apple must compote, peel the apples, remove the core and cut into wedges. Bring the must with sugar, cloves, cinnamon and lemon juice to the boil and let the apple wedges steep in it until they are soft but still firm to the bite.

2. Pour the apple cider compote into a suitable container, close tightly and store in a cool and dark place.

18. Raspberry Coconut Tart

ingredients

- 50 g raspberries (frozen)
- Coconut chips (or desiccated coconut)
- 75 g coconut oil
- 80 g butter (salted)
- 2 tbsp cocoa powder (raw)
- 2-3 tbsp rice syrup

preparation

1. Line a large deep plate or cake tin with baking paper for the raspberry and coconut tart (a plate is ideal because the indentation creates a good shape).
2. Scatter the berries and coconut chips on the plate. Melt coconut oil and butter in a

pan or in the microwave (the coconut oil takes longer, so add the butter a little later).

3. Stir in the cocoa powder and syrup, pour over the berries and coconut chips and let set in the refrigerator for thirty minutes.

4. To serve, either break into pieces or cut with a knife like a cake.

19. Chia brownie

ingredients

- 300 g chocolate (milk and butter)
- 100 g margarine (semi-fat)
- 100 g almonds (ground)
- 10 g sprinkle sweetness
- 5 eggs
- 3 tbsp chia seeds
- 100 g dark chocolate (for the topping)
- Pinch of salt

preparation

1. For the chia brownie, melt the chocolate with the margarine over steam. Mix the almonds with the chia and salt, mix the eggs and the powdered sugar with a mixer, but

make sure that it doesn't get frothy, stir in the chocolate and almond mixture.

2. Empty into a baking pan lined with baking paper with a rim and bake in the preheated (180 °) oven for about 20 minutes. Let cool and glaze with the melted chocolate. After the glaze has set, cut the chia brownie into pieces.

20. Blackberry layered yogurt

ingredients

- 250 g blackberry
- 500 g yogurt (1.5% fat)
- 60 g pistachio kernels (4 tbsp)
- 4 tsp honey

Preparation steps

1. Sort the blackberries and place 150 g in a tall container.
2. Add half of the yoghurt and puree finely with a hand blender.
3. Divide the blackberry yogurt between 4 glasses.

4. Pour the rest of the yogurt into the glasses. Arrange the remaining blackberries on top.
5. Roughly chop the pistachio nuts and mix with the honey. Pour the layered yoghurt and serve.

21. Poached pears

ingredients

- 1 organic orange
- 400 ml white wine
- 100 g honey
- 50 g cane sugar
- 1 rod cinnamon
- 0.1 g saffron threads (1 packet)
- 800 g pears (4 pears)

Preparation steps

O Rinse orange with hot, rub dry and cut into slices.

1   Bring the wine, honey, sugar, orange slices, cinnamon and saffron to a boil with 200 ml of water in a saucepan.

2   In the meantime, peel the pears. Cut out the flower bases and "straighten" the pears on the bottom so that they can stand.

3   Skim off the foam on the brew. Put the pears in vertically. Weigh down with a plate so that the pears stay below the surface of the brew. Let simmer (poach) for 30 minutes over medium heat just below boiling point. Take the pears off the heat and let them cool in the liquid. So that the pears absorb the aroma evenly, put the fruit in the brew for at least 24 hours. Serve the drained pears with a little maple syrup and sweetened yogurt.

22. Vanilla chilli pineapple

ingredients

- 1 pineapple (fresh, whole)
- 300 g cane sugar (brown)
- 300 ml pineapple juice
- 100 ml of mango juice
- 1 chilli pepper (red)
- 1 vanilla pod

preparation

0 For the vanilla chilli pineapple, peel the pineapple and cut into cubes. Halve and core the chilli pepper.

1 Put the brown cane sugar in a saucepan and wait until it starts to caramelize. As soon as it starts, gradually stir in the pineapple juice and mango juice. Halve the vanilla pod, scrape it out

and stir into the pineapple mixture. Add the half chilli peppers and let everything simmer for about 10 minutes.

2   Remove the chilli pepper from the pineapple compote and divide everything into bowls and let them cool well in the refrigerator. Garnish with chilli threads and serve the vanilla chilli pineapple.

23. peach pie

ingredients

- 400 g flour type 1050
- 1 packet baking powder
- 1 pinch salt
- 150 g
- cane sugar
- 350 ml buttermilk
- eggs
- 1200 g ripe, firm peaches
- 50 g almond sticks
- 1 packet vanilla sugar

Preparation steps

0 Mix the flour, baking powder, salt and half of the sugar in a bowl.
1 Whisk the buttermilk and eggs together. Pour slowly onto the flour mixture and mix briefly with the hand mixer to form a smooth dough.
2 Line a baking sheet with parchment paper. Put the dough on top and spread it evenly with a rubber spatula.

3   Wash the peaches, pat dry, cut in half, stone and cut into wedges. Distribute evenly on the dough.
4   Scatter the almond sticks, remaining sugar and vanilla sugar on top. Bake in the preheated oven at 180 ° C (fan oven: 160 ° C, gas: level 2-3) on the middle rack for 25-30 minutes.

24. Caramel creme brulee

ingredients

- 200 ml whipped cream
- 300 ml of milk
- 150 g caramel candies
- yolks
- 60 g sugar (brown)

preparation

0 For the caramel crème brûlée, first bring the whipped cream, milk and sweets to the boil and stir until the sweets have dissolved. Let cool a little and stir in the yolks.

1 Chill for at least 3 hours.

2 Preheat the oven to 95 ° C before using it again. Pour the cream into ovenproof molds. Put in the oven for about 1 hour until the cream has set and has a thin skin.
3 Chill well in the refrigerator again.
4 Sprinkle with the sugar and caramelize the caramel crème brûlée briefly.

25. Avocado cream with honey

ingredients

- egg yolks
- tbsp honey
- 250 g low-fat curd cheese
- 2 pieces avocado (ripe)
- 1 lemon (juice)
- 2 pieces of egg whites
- 1 pinch of salt
- 1/2 bunch of lemon balm

preparation

O For the avocado cream with honey, beat the egg yolks with the honey in a bowl until frothy and add the skimmed curd spoon by spoon.

1   Halve the avocados lengthways, remove the stone and scrape out the pulp with a spoon. Puree with the lemon juice in a blender and mix into the curd and egg mixture.

2   Beat the egg whites with the pinch of salt until very stiff and fold them carefully into the honey and avocado cream.

3   Wash off the lemon balm and pluck the leaves off. Put some very nice leaves aside, cut the rest into narrow strips and mix with the cream.

4   The avocado cream with honey spread on dessert bowls, garnish with the remaining lemon and serve immediately.

26. Tropical fruit salad with coconut

ingredients

- 200 g half papaya (1 half papaya)
- 300 g small mango (1 small mango)
- 125 g physalis
- 700 g medium pineapple (1 medium pineapple)
- 1 kiwi
- 1 lime
- tbsp broad desiccated coconut
- 150 g coconut yogurt
- 2 tbsp milk (1.5% fat)

Preparation steps

0 Peel and core the papaya, peel the mango and
   cut the pulp from the stone. Cut both fruits
   into bite-sized pieces.

1 Remove the physalis from the parchment skins, wash and cut in half.
2 Peel and quarter the pineapple and cut out the stalk. Cut the pulp into bite-sized pieces.
3 Peel the kiwi and cut into pieces. Halve the lime, squeeze out and measure 2-3 tablespoons of juice. Mix all the fruit pieces with the lime juice, leave to stand for 20 minutes.
4 Roast the desiccated coconut in a pan without fat until light brown.
5 Before serving, beat the coconut yoghurt and milk with the hand mixer or a whisk until frothy.
6 Spread the coconut sauce over the salad and sprinkle with the roasted desiccated coconut.

27. Baked apple muffins

ingredients

- 240 g flour
- 100 g granulated sugar
- 10 g sugar (brown)
- 1 teaspoon baking powder
- 1/2 teaspoon baking soda
- 1 pinch of salt
- eggs (beaten)
- 110 g butter (soft)
- 1 teaspoon vanilla pulp
- 100 g baked apple jam
- 40 g marzipan (alternative for marzipan lovers)
- 1/2 teaspoon cinnamon

preparation

1. For the baked apple muffins, preheat the oven to 180 degrees and place the paper molds in the muffin tray.
2. In a bowl, combine the flour, sugar, baking powder, baking soda and salt.
3. In a second bowl, mix the eggs, baked apple jam , butter and vanilla pulp and, if desired, the grated marzipan.
4. Carefully fold in the damp mixture into the flour mixture. Use a spoon to pour the dough into the paper molds and bake on the middle rack for about 20 minutes.
5. Allow the baked apple muffins to cool before consuming.

28. Banana Tiramisu

ingredients

- eggs
- 1 cup of mascarpone
- 1/4 l whipped cream
- tbsp granulated sugar
- vanilla sugar
- 1 1/2 Pkg. Ladyfingers
- cocoa
- 4-6 pieces of bananas

preparation

- For the banana tiramisu, separate the egg white from the yolk.

- Mix the yolks with sugar and mascarpone, add the whipped cream (previously beaten until stiff) and vanilla sugar.
- Dip the ladyfingers in cocoa and place in a rectangular shape.
- Put a layer of cream on top, add the bananas, then another layer of cream until the ingredients are used up.

29. Baked apple in red wine

ingredients

- 1/4 l red wine
- tbsp sugar
- stick (s) cinnamon
- cloves
- apples
- Butter flakes
- Wine
- Cranberry jam

preparation

- For the baked apple, bring to the boil in red wine with red wine, sugar, cinnamon sticks and cloves. Remove the core from the apples and flatten slightly at the bottom. Cover with flakes of butter and place in a well-greased, fire-proof dish. Fry in the oven at 200 ° C for about 20 minutes.

- Pour wine over the apples and fill them with cranberry jam. Continue frying for another 10 minutes, pouring the liquid over them several times. Serve the baked apple in red wine hot with the red wine sauce.

30. Raspberry Amaretto Tiramisu

ingredients

- 1/2 pod of vanilla
- 80 ml of milk
- 1 egg yolk
- tbsp sugar
- 100 g mascarino
- 60 ml cream (whipped)
- 150 g raspberries
- 2 tbsp icing sugar
- 20 ml amaretto (almond liqueur)
- some ladyfingers
- Raspberries (for the garnish)
- Icing sugar (for sprinkling)
- Mint (for garnish)

preparation

- Cut the vanilla pod lengthways and scrape out the pulp. Put the vanilla pulp with the milk, egg yolk and the sugar in a saucepan and mix until smooth with a hand blender.
- Briefly heat the mixture, stirring constantly, until the egg yolk binds the mass easily. Then stir in the mascarino and fold in the whipped cream.
- Now puree the raspberries with icing sugar and amaretto to make a sauce. Break the sponge fingers into small pieces and soak them in the raspberry sauce.
- Place a ring shape with a diameter of 10 cm on a plate. Place the biscuit pieces as a base in it. Spread half of the cream on top and place some raspberries on top as a decoration.
- Lift off the ring shape, sprinkle the raspberry tiramisu with icing sugar and garnish with mint.

31. Crunchy chocolate pralines

ingredients

- 200 g dark chocolate
- 40 g muesli flake mix
- 100 g flakes made from spelled
- 25 g cherries (dried, unsweetened)

Preparation steps

1. Fill a saucepan with water, bring to the boil and then turn the stove to the lowest setting.
2. Finely chop the dark chocolate and place about two thirds of it in a bowl. Put the bowl

in the saucepan and carefully melt the couverture in a water bath. Stir occasionally.

3. As soon as the chocolate is completely melted, remove the bowl from the heat, add the remaining chocolate, and slowly stir until everything is melted.

4. In a large bowl, carefully mix the muesli mixture, spelled flakes, dried cherries, and melted chocolate to cover everything covered with chocolate.

5. Shape around 30 chocolate pralines with two teaspoons and place on baking paper. Then let it dry for about 2-3 hours in a cool environment.

32. Raw blueberry cheesecake

ingredients

- 300 g almond kernels (unpeeled)
- 200 g dried date (pitted)
- 450 g cashew nuts (soaked overnight)
- 50 ml agave syrup
- 150 g coconut oil
- 1 tsp vanilla powder
- 1 lemon (juice)
- tbsp desiccated coconut
- 50 g blueberries (frozen)
- 50 g blueberries (fresh)

Preparation steps

0 For the Raw Blueberry Cheesecake base, place
   the almonds and dates in a powerful food

processor and mix to form a "dough base". Add water or vegetable milk as desired and depending on the stickiness of the mixture.

1 Put the finished dough base mass into a freezer-safe dish (for example 26 x 20 centimeters) and press firmly. Place in the freezer.

2 Now put the cashew nuts soaked overnight with agave syrup, melted coconut oil, vanilla pulp, and lemon juice in a food processor and puree to a creamy mass.

3 Halve the cashew mixture. Mix one half with 3 tablespoons of desiccated coconut, put the other half in a food processor again and puree with the frozen blueberries.

4 Take the dough base out of the freezer and first brush with the light cashew coconut mixture. Then spread some fresh blueberries on top and cover with the cashew-blueberry mixture. Garnish with other blueberries if you like or add them to serving.

5 Place the raw blueberry cheesecake in the freezer for about 30 minutes. Take the blueberry cheesecake out of the freezer about 10 minutes before serving and garnish the

remaining 2 tablespoons of desiccated coconut and the remaining blueberries.

33. Chocolate Popsicles

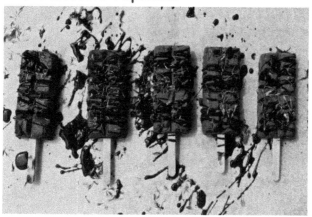

ingredients

- dates
- 1 banana
- 200 ml almond drink (almond milk)
- 80 ml coconut milk
- tsp cocoa powder + something for decoration
- cocoa nibs

Preparation steps

1. Put all the other ingredients except for the cocoa nibs in a blender and puree them finely. Fill the popsicle molds, put the stalks directly

into the ice cream, or let the ice cream freeze for about 20 minutes and then add the stalks.

2. Let the ice cream freeze for at least 4 hours and then sprinkle with a little cocoa powder and cocoa nibs and serve immediately!

34. Breakfast muffins with blueberries

ingredients

- 30 g coconut oil (2 tbsp)
- 175 g wholemeal spelled flour
- 1 heaped teaspoon
- baking powder
- 1 pinch salt
- eggs
- 150 ml almond drink (almond milk)
- 1 banana
- 125 g blueberries
- sugar-free jam or birch powdered sugar for garnish

Preparation steps

1. Melt coconut oil in a saucepan. In the meantime, mix the flour, baking powder and salt in a bowl.
2. Whisk eggs in a bowl and mix with coconut oil and almond milk. Add everything to the flour mixture and process into a smooth dough with a hand mixer.
3. Mash the banana with a fork. Wash and drain blueberries. Fold both under the dough.
4. Line the muffin tray with muffin molds and distribute the batter evenly over the hollows. Bake the muffins in the preheated oven on the middle rack at 190 ° C (convection 170 ° C; gas: level 2-3) for about 25 minutes.
5. Garnish the muffins with chia jam or birch powdered sugar, if you like.

35. Pumpkin Cheesecake

ingredients

- 800 g hokkaido pumpkin (1 hokkaido pumpkin)
- 100 g whole grain shortbread biscuits
- 50 g walnuts
- 50 g butter
- 300 g cream cheese (50% fat in dry matter)
- tbsp maple syrup
- eggs
- 1 pinch salt
- $\frac{1}{2}$ tsp cinnamon
- $\frac{1}{2}$ tsp ginger
- 1 pinch nutmeg
- 200 g sour cream
- 1 tsp vanilla powder

Preparation steps

1. Line the bottom of a springform pan with parchment paper.
2. Cut the pumpkin into four pieces, remove the seeds and bake in the oven at 180 ° C (convection 160 ° C; gas: level 2-3) for about 40-45 minutes until the flesh is soft.
3. In the meantime, place the shortbread biscuits in a freezer bag and crumble them with a rolling pin or briefly chop them up with a mixer. Chop the walnuts and add a few to decorate. Melt the butter and add to the biscuit and nut mix.
4. Remove the pulp from the slightly cooled pumpkin with a tablespoon and puree in a bowl with the hand blender.
5. Whip cream cheese with maple syrup, eggs and spices until creamy. Then fold in the pumpkin puree and spread the mixture on the biscuit base.
6. Bake the pumpkin pie for 50 minutes at the same temperature. Then take it out and let it cool for about an hour.
7. For the topping, mix the sour cream and vanilla with the mixer until creamy and distribute on the cooled pumpkin pie. Then put again in the oven for 10 minutes.

8. Chill the pumpkin cheesecake before serving.

36. Energy balls

ingredients

- ½ orange
- 50 g oatmeal
- 75 g dried dates
- 50 g almond kernels
- 20 g honey (2 tbsp)
- tbsp sesame

Preparation steps

1. Squeeze half of the orange. Mix oatmeal and 2 tablespoons of orange juice in a bowl.

2. Cut the date in half, cut it with stones, and chop it into lightning choppers with almonds. Probably add a tablespoon of orange juice.
3. Mix the date and almond mixture well with honey to make oat flakes.
4. Toast the sesame seeds in a hot, fat-free pan over medium heat for 3 minutes. Transfer to a small plate and let cool.
5. The mixture of date and almonds is molded into 28 balls of approximately the same size (about 2 cm in diameter) and rolled one after another in roasted sesame seeds.
6. Line the baking sheet with parchment paper, distribute the balls on it and let it dry for at least 1 hour. We provide 7 energy balls per serving.

37. Sweet pumpkin waffles

ingredients

- 200 g wholemeal spelled flour
- 1 tbsp baking powder
- 1 pinch salt
- 1 tsp cinnamon
- 1 vanilla pod (pulp)
- eggs (size m)
- 160 ml milk (1.5% fat) (alternatively plant milk)
- 150 g pumpkin puree
- 2 tbsp maple syrup (more for garnish if needed)

Preparation steps

1. Mix whole spelled flour, baking powder, salt, cinnamon, and a vanilla pod pulp in a large bowl.
2. In another bowl, beat the eggs until frothy. Then mix the milk, then the pumpkin puree and the maple syrup with the egg foam.
3. Now add the egg and pumpkin mixture to the flour mixture and stir thoroughly.
4. Preheat the waffle iron. Then, depending on the size of the appliance, pour about two tablespoons of batter into the center of the hot waffle iron, close the lid and bake until golden brown in about three to five minutes.
5. Serve the finished pumpkin waffles drizzled with maple syrup as desired.

38. Banana Pecan Bread

ingredients

- 1 cube yeast
- 450 g whole wheat flour
- 1 pinch salt
- bananas
- 200 g pecans
- tbsp rapeseed oil

Preparation steps

1. Crumble the yeast and mix with 5 tbsp lukewarm water.
2. Mix 400 g flour and 1 pinch of salt in a bowl. Make a well in the middle and add the yeast. Dust with a little flour and cover and let rise for 15 minutes.

3. In the meantime, peel the bananas and mash them with a fork. Roughly chop half of the nuts.

4. Gradually add the bananas and nuts with 2 tablespoons of oil and approx. 140 ml of lukewarm water to the flour and work into a smooth dough. Cover and let rise in a warm place for about 1 hour.

5. Brush a loaf pan (approx. 30 cm long) with the rest of the oil and dust with a little flour. Knead the dough again and pour it into the loaf pan. Cover with the remaining nuts and cover again for 15 minutes.

6. Bake bread in a preheated oven at 160 ° C (convection 140 ° C; gas: level 1-2) for about 1 hour. Then fall out of the mold and let cool down.

39. Date cake with mango

ingredients

- 100 g fresh dates
- eggs
- tbsp rapeseed oil
- 100 g low-fat quark
- 160 g whole wheat flour (e.g. whole wheat or spelled flour)
- 1 ½ tsp baking powder
- 1 tsp cinnamon
- 450 g ripe mango (1 ripe mango)
- 10 g butter (2 teaspoons)

Preparation steps

1. Halve the dates, stone them and place in a large mixing bowl. Puree finely with a hand blender.
2. Add the eggs, oil and low-fat quark and stir everything with the whisk of a hand mixer until creamy
3. Mix the flour with the baking powder and cinnamon in another bowl. Sift into the date cream and stir in. If the dough is very firm, mix in a little water if necessary.
4. Wash and peel the mango, cut the pulp into slices from the stone and dice.
5. Grease a small rectangular baking dish (approx. 27 x 18 cm) with butter. Pour in the dough and smooth it out with a spatula.
6. Spread the mango cubes on top and bake the cake in the preheated oven at 180 ° C (convection 160 ° C; gas: level 2-3) on the middle rack for 35–40 minutes. Take out and let cool in the mold. Then cut into 10 equal pieces, lift out of the mold and serve.

40. Date Cookies with ginger

ingredients

- 350 g fresh dates (30 fresh dates)
- 125 g peeled almond kernels
- 50 g millet
- ½ organic orange
- g ginger (1 piece)
- eggs
- 50 g wheat meal

Preparation steps

1. Stone and finely chop the dates.
2. Roughly chop the almonds.
3. Finely grind millet in a blitz chopper.
4. Rinse half an orange with hot water and rub dry. Rub the peel finely.

5. Ginger peel and finely chop.
6. Mix the dates, almonds, orange peel and ginger.
7. Separate eggs. Beat egg whites with 1 tablespoon of cold water until very stiff. Stir in egg yolks one at a time.
8. Add the date mixture, millet and crushed wheat and fold in carefully.
9. Place the dough tablespoon at a time on 2 baking sheets lined with baking paper. Bake one after the other in the preheated oven at 150 ° C (gas: setting 1-2) on the middle shelf for 10-15 minutes until light brown; Bake both trays simultaneously in a convection oven at 130 ° C. Cool on a wire rack.

41. Coconut milk rice with blueberries

ingredients

- 500 ml milk (1.5% fat)
- 20 g sugar (1 tbsp)
- 10 g vanilla sugar (1 teaspoon)
- 200 g rice pudding
- 150 g blueberries
- 20 g desiccated coconut (2 tbsp)
- g powdered sugar (1 teaspoon)

Preparation steps

1. Boil milk, sugar and vanilla sugar in a pan. Cover with rice and simmer over medium heat for about 25 minutes, stirring occasionally.
2. In the meantime, wash the blueberries and tap them to dry. Roast the dried coconut in a fat-free pan over medium heat until golden.
3. Divide the rice pudding into 6 bowls and serve with blueberries, powdered sugar and dried coconut.

42. Cottage cheese muffins with strawberries

ingredients

- 1 organic lemon
- eggs
- 70 g coconut blossom sugar
- salt
- 400 g low-fat quark
- 70 g creme fraiche cheese
- 30 g cornstarch (2 tbsp)
- 250 g strawberries
- ½ packet clear cake topping
- 125 ml apple juice

Preparation steps

1. Rinse lemon with hot water, rub dry and finely grate the peel. Halve and squeeze the lemon.

2. Put the eggs and 1 tbsp lemon juice in a mixing bowl. Briefly whip with the whisk of a hand mixer. Add coconut blossom sugar and a pinch of salt and whip for another 3 minutes until creamy.
3. Drain the quark, then add the crème fraîche and the grated lemon zest and stir in. Add the starch by the tablespoon and stir in briefly.
4. Line a muffin tin (12 hollows) with paper liners. Pour in the quark mixture and smooth it out with a rubber spatula. Place the muffin tray on the oven rack and bake on the middle rack in the preheated oven at 200 ° C (fan oven: 180 ° C, gas: level 3) for about 15 minutes.
5. Let the oven cool down with the door slightly open. Then place the muffins in the paper cases on a wire rack and cool completely in about 45 minutes.
6. In the meantime, carefully wash the strawberries, drain them, clean them and cut them lengthways into slices.
7. Put the icing powder in a small saucepan. Gradually stir in the apple juice with a whisk and bring to a boil.
8. Spread half of the hot cake icing on the cooled muffins. Cover the muffins with strawberry

slices, drizzle with the remaining cake topping and let the fruit set for about 20 minutes.

43. Cream cheese yogurt cake with biscuit base

ingredients

- 150 g whole grain shortbread biscuits
- 125 g yogurt butter
- sheets gelatin
- 1 lemon
- 500 g cream cheese (13% fat)
- 400 g yogurt (1.5% fat)
- 125 ml orange juice
- 50 g whole cane sugar
- 1 handful fresh fruit at will

Preparation steps

1. Put the biscuits in a large freezer bag. Seal the bag and crumble the contents completely with your hands or a meat tenderizer.

2. Line a spring from with parchment paper. Melt the butter in a small saucepan, mix with the breadcrumbs, and press firmly into the springform pan with your hands or spoon.
3. Soak gelatin sheets in cold water for about 5 minutes. Squeeze the lemon and measure out 2 tablespoons of juice.
4. Mix the cream cheese, yoghurt and lemon juice with the hand mixer.
5. Heat the orange juice and sugar in a saucepan while stirring until the sugar dissolves. Remove from heat and dissolve the squeezed gelatin in it.
6. Stir the gelatine and juice mix into the cream cheese mixture.
7. Place the cream cheese cream on the crumbly base in the springform pan and cool the cream cheese cake for at least 3 hours. Garnish with fresh fruit if you like before serving.

44. Raspberry jelly

ingredients

- 12 sheetsn white gelatin
- 1 organic lemon
- stems lemon balm
- 650 g raspberries
- 700 ml prosecco or light grape juice
- 50 g cane sugar

Preparation steps

1. Soak the gelatine in cold water for at least 5 minutes.
2. Line a bowl or terrine dish with a capacity of approx. 1.2 l with cling film.
3. Rinse and dry the lemon and grate the peel finely. Squeeze the lemon.

4. Wash lemon balm, shake dry, pluck leaves and cut into fine strips.
5. Sort the raspberries, mix very carefully with the lemon peel and lemon balm.
6. Put the raspberries in the mold.
7. Mix the prosecco and lemon juice.
8. Remove approx. 100 ml and bring to the boil in a saucepan with the sugar while stirring.
9. Squeeze out the gelatine. Take the saucepan off the stove and dissolve the gelatine in the hot liquid.
10. Add the gelatin mixture to the rest of the prosecco and stir.
11. Pour liquid into the mold. Hit the shape a few times on the work surface so that everything mixes well. Chill the brawn for about 4 hours.
12. Before serving, briefly put the mold in hot water to loosen the brawn from the edges. Then turn the brawn out of the mold, remove the foil and cut the brawn into slices with a warm knife. Lemon sorbet goes well with it.

45. Strawberry espresso layered dish

ingredients

- 250 g strawberries
- 1 small lemon
- tbsp apple syrup
- 1 small organic orange
- 250 g lowfat quark
- $\frac{1}{2}$ tsp vanilla powder
- 100 g cantuccini
- tbsp espresso (cooled)

Preparation steps

1. Carefully wash the strawberries in a bowl of water, pat dry with kitchen paper and clean. Halve or quarter depending on the size.
2. Halve and squeeze the lemon. Put the berries in a second bowl, mix in the apple syrup and 1

teaspoon lemon juice. Cover and leave to stand for 20 minutes (marinate).

3. In the meantime, wash the orange, rub it dry and grate the peel finely. Then halve the orange and squeeze out the juice.
4. Put the quark in a bowl. Add the orange peel, vanilla powder and 1 tbsp lemon juice.
5. Mix in enough orange juice with a whisk so that the quark becomes smooth and creamy.
6. Break the cantuccini into medium-sized pieces, divide between 4 glasses and sprinkle evenly with the espresso. Layer alternately with orange quark and strawberries and serve.

46. Mustard and strawberry trifle

ingredients

- 250 g strawberries
- 60 g of sugar
- 250 ml Rama Cremefine for whipping
- 1 packet of vanilla sugar
- Sponge cake base (finished product)
- 1 teaspoon curry
- 1 tbsp balsamic vinegar
- 1/2 - 1 teaspoon mustard
- 1 teaspoon honey

preparation

1. Wash and clean the strawberries and, depending on the size, quarter or halve.

Sprinkle with the sugar and let the juice steep for 30 minutes.

2. In the meantime, beat the cremefine and vanilla sugar with the whisk of a hand mixer and chill.

3. With a glass, the dessert will later be served, cut out 8 circles from the sponge cake base.

4. Pour off the juice from the strawberries and collect, season with balsamic vinegar, mustard and honey and add to the strawberries again.

5. Layer the strawberries, sponge cake and cremefine in the glass, starting with strawberries and cremefine .

47. Asparagus panna cotta

ingredients

Raspberry pulp:

- 100 g raspberries
- 25 g sugar (or honey)
- 1/2 sheet of gelatin

Asparagus panna cotta:

- 50 g asparagus (white)
- 1/2 pod of vanilla
- 175 g cream (liquid)
- 175 g milk
- 50 grams of sugar
- 2.5-3 sheets of gelatin

preparation

1. For the raspberry pulp, boil the berries with sugar or honey and mix.
2. Add the soaked gelatine while it is still warm and fill the raspberry pulp into dariol dishes.
3. In the meantime, peel the asparagus for the asparagus panna cotta , cut into small pieces and slowly cook until soft with half of the cream, the scraped out vanilla pod and the sugar.
4. Mix well in the kitchen mixer.
5. Add the soaked gelatine and dissolve in it.
6. Strain the mixture and mix it with the rest of the milk and cream.
7. Allow the mixture to cool briefly and carefully pour onto the cooled raspberry pulp so that the pulp does not mix with the asparagus milk.
8. Now chill the asparagus panna cotta for approx. 1-1.5 hours before serving.

48. Blueberry Banana Muffins

ingredients

- 1 small organic lemon
- 200 g wheat flour type 1050
- tbsp wheat bran
- tsp baking powder
- 80 g coconut blossom sugar
- 1 pinch salt
- 150 ml milk (1.5% fat)
- 1 egg
- 2 tbsp rapeseed oil
- 250 g ripe small bananas (2 ripe small bananas)
- 175 g blueberries

Preparation steps

1. Rinse the lemon with hot water, rub dry and rub the peel. Put the flour, bran, baking powder, coconut blossom sugar and a pinch of salt in a bowl. Mix everything thoroughly.
2. Mix the milk, egg and oil in a second bowl with a whisk until smooth. Add to the flour mixture and stir everything into a smooth dough.
3. Peel the bananas and finely mash them with a fork. Add the banana puree to the batter and stir in thoroughly.
4. Sort the blueberries, add to the batter and fold in carefully.
5. Line a coated muffin tin (for 12 muffins) with paper baking cases. Divide the dough into the molds.
6. Bake the muffins in the preheated oven at 200 ° C (convection: 180 ° C, gas: level 3) for about 30 minutes. Prick the center of a muffin with a wooden stick: if it comes out clean, the muffins are ready; otherwise bake for a few more minutes.
7. Remove the muffins from the tin with the paper liners. Let cool on a wire rack for at least 5 minutes and serve lukewarm or cold.

49. Avocado sorbet with marinated strawberries

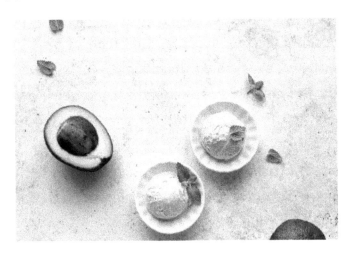

ingredients

- pieces avocado
- tbsp lime juice
- 250 ml cane sugar syrup
- 2 pieces of egg whites
- 1 teaspoon lime zest
- 250 g strawberries
- 1 tbsp sugar
- tbsp orange juice

preparation

1. For the avocado sorbet with marinated strawberries, halve the avocados, remove the stones and scrape out the pulp with a spoon.

2. Puree with 2 tbsp lime juice and the sugar syrup.
3. Beat the egg white until stiff and mix into the cream and the lime zest and season with lime juice.
4. Pour the sorbet mixture into a shallow bowl and freeze for 4 hours, stirring once every half an hour.
5. Wash, clean and slice the strawberries.
6. Mix with sugar and orange juice and marinate for at least 30 minutes.
7. For the avocado sorbet with marinated strawberries, spread the strawberry ragout on plates and serve two scoops of sorbet on each.

50. raspberry cream

ingredients

- 200 g raspberries
- tbsp icing sugar
- eggs
- 100 g of icing sugar
- 1 packet of vanilla sugar
- 500 ml white wine
- sheets of gelatin
- 250 ml whipped cream
- 1 shot of raspberry spirit
- 1/2 lemon (juice)
- Raspberries

preparation

1. Mix the raspberries with icing sugar, bring to the boil and strain through a sieve.
2. Beat eggs with icing sugar, vanilla sugar and white wine over the steam until frothy, remove from the fire and continue beating until the mixture has cooled down.
3. Dissolve the gelatine, whip the whipped cream until stiff and fold into the egg mixture with

the raspberry spirit, lemon juice and raspberry puree.

4. Half fill the dessert glasses, fill with raspberries and spread the rest of the cream on top.

5. Serve well chilled.

CONCLUSION

Remember that the dessert should be consumed in moderation, that is, only a small portion should eat a balanced diet and avoid gaining weight.

Lightning Source UK Ltd.
Milton Keynes UK
UKHW021147110821
388616UK00007B/65